Fantastic Fairs

County Fair

by Julie Murray

Dash!
LEVELED READERS
An Imprint of Abdo Zoom • abdobooks.com

3

3 Dash!
LEVELED READERS

Level 1 – Beginning
Short and simple sentences with familiar words or patterns for children who are beginning to understand how letters and sounds go together.

Level 2 – Emerging
Longer words and sentences with more complex language patterns for readers who are practicing common words and letter sounds.

Level 3 – Transitional
More developed language and vocabulary for readers who are becoming more independent.

THIS BOOK CONTAINS RECYCLED MATERIALS

abdobooks.com

Published by Abdo Zoom, a division of ABDO, PO Box 398166, Minneapolis, Minnesota 55439.
Copyright © 2020 by Abdo Consulting Group, Inc. International copyrights reserved in all countries.
No part of this book may be reproduced in any form without written permission from the publisher.
Dash!™ is a trademark and logo of Abdo Zoom.

Printed in the United States of America, North Mankato, Minnesota.
052019
092019

Photo Credits: Alamy, Getty Images, iStock, Shutterstock, © Martybiniasz p6 / CC BY-SA 4.0
Production Contributors: Kenny Abdo, Jennie Forsberg, Grace Hansen, John Hansen
Design Contributors: Dorothy Toth, Neil Klinepier

Library of Congress Control Number: 2018963308

Publisher's Cataloging in Publication Data

Names: Murray, Julie, author.
Title: County fair / by Julie Murray.
Description: Minneapolis, Minnesota : Abdo Zoom, 2020 | Series: Fantastic fairs |
    Includes online resources and index.
Identifiers: ISBN 9781532127236 (lib. bdg.) | ISBN 9781532128219 (ebook) |
    ISBN 9781532128707 (Read-to-me ebook)
Subjects: LCSH: County fairs--Juvenile literature. | Agricultural fairs--Juvenile
    literature. | Fairs--Juvenile literature.
Classification: DDC 394.6--dc23

Table of Contents

County Fair

Many people can join in the fun at the county fair! There is something for everyone to enjoy, like eating yummy foods, going on rides, and seeing animals!

The Midway

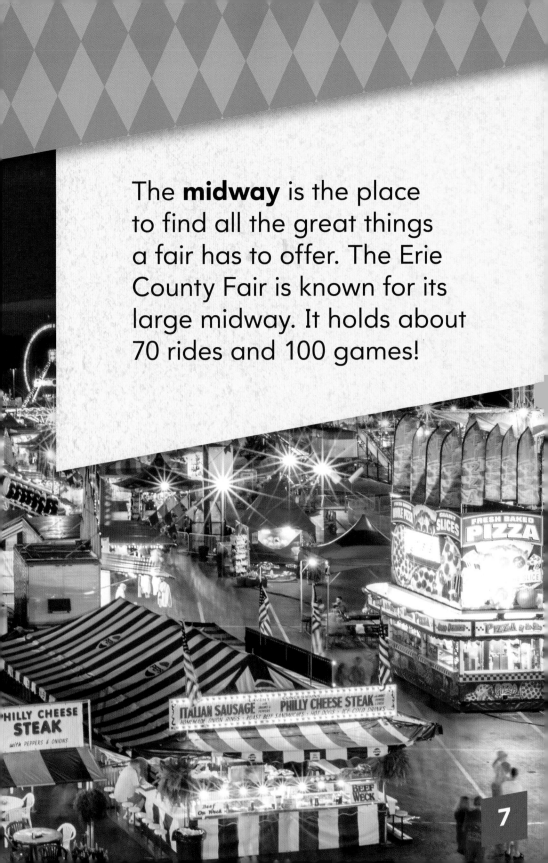

The **midway** is the place to find all the great things a fair has to offer. The Erie County Fair is known for its large midway. It holds about 70 rides and 100 games!

County fairs have many rides. The Ferris wheel, merry-go-round, and giant swings are favorites. Some county fairs even have small roller coasters.

ONE PRIZE
PER DAY
PER PLAYER

County fairs also have plenty of games. The ring toss and balloon darts are both popular. Players can win stuffed animals and fun toys.

Food is another big part of the fair. Corn dogs, French fries, and mini donuts are aplenty. Local foods are often served too. Roasted corn on the cob is a great choice.

Agriculture and Animals

Many county fairs have an **agricultural show**. Farming equipment, past and present, is on display. There are also tractor pulls and farming demonstrations.

There is usually a **livestock** barn at a county fair. This is where you can see cattle, sheep, and pigs. **4-H** is a big part of the fair. Kids can win prizes for the livestock they have raised.

Food contests are a big part of the fair too. There are pie-baking, jam-making, and pumpkin-growing contests. The winners take home a blue ribbon!

19

The All-Alaskan Racing Pigs travel to county fairs around the country. A fun ride and a yummy treat to follow the races makes for a great day!

More Facts

- The San Diego County Fair is the largest county fair in the US. More than 1.5 million people attend it each year.

- The Jefferson County Fair in New York is the longest consecutive running fair in the US. It began in 1817 as the Jefferson County Agricultural Society.

- The Rice County Fair in Minnesota has an Unusual Vegetable Competition. Contestants win prizes for their oddly-shaped produce.

Glossary

4-H – a US-based network of youth organizations whose mission is to engage youth to help them reach their fullest potential. Programs having to do with agriculture, science, engineering, technology, and more are available.

agricultural show – a public event showing the equipment, animals, and recreation related to agriculture and raising livestock.

livestock – cows, horses, sheep or other animals raised or kept on a farm or ranch.

midway – the area or strip where food stands, shows, and games are found at fairs.

Index

Online Resources

Booklinks
NONFICTION NETWORK
FREE! ONLINE NONFICTION RESOURCES

To learn more about county fairs, please visit **abdobooklinks.com** or scan this QR code. These links are routinely monitored and updated to provide the most current information available.